楊　貴　妃
YANG KUEI-FEI
The Most Famous Beauty of China

BY

SHU-CHIUNG

(Mrs Wu Lien-teh)

Dedicated

TO THE MEMORY OF MY DEAR SISTER

TUAN-CHIUNG

(The late Mrs. Lim Boon-keng)

ABOUT THE AUTHOR . . . . . .

Born into a distinguished family in 1882, Shu-chiung was one of the first Singapore girls to receive a Western education. Her appreciation and command of the English language matched her deep love of Chinese history and literature, and the fruits of this happy 'marriage' between the East and West were three sensitive and elegant historical romances, written in English, on three of the most famous heroines of ancient China.

An invalid for much of her later life, Shu-chiung researched and wrote from her sick bed in Peking, where she lived with her eminent husband, Dr. Wu Lien-teh, who was in China at the special request of the government to combat the pneumonic plague which ravaged Manchuria.

Shu-chiung's intention had been to compose four books on the four most famous heroines of China: Yang Kuei-fei, the most artful; Hsi Shih, the most beautiful; Chao Chun, the most virtuous; Tiao Chan, the most patriotic. Sadly, she died before the fourth volume was completed, but she has given us three beautiful and historically accurate portrayals, of which *Yang Kuei-fei* is the first.

PREFACE

The story of Yang Kuei-fei is well known to the main body of Chinese throughout the country. The literary classes have access to a vast popular literature extending over hundreds of years, while the less educated remember it as they do other events of their long national history from visits to their village and metropolitan theatres. In fact, Yang Kuei-fei is as familiar a stage as a historical character, and the ambition of every Chinese actress to play the part of this famous beauty may be compared to that of many European and American actresses in attempting the rôle of one of Shakespeare's great heroines, like Juliet or Desdemona.

Yang Kuei-fei lived in the time of the Tang dynasty (A.D. 618–905), and for over twenty years was undisputed mistress of the imperial court. Her beauty was said to be unsurpassed, her vivacity unrivalled, and her talents as a musician, singer and dancer were unexcelled. It must be remembered that the accomplishments of a lady in those days were many and complex. Every girl aspiring to shine in society had to learn to sing, dance, play music, compose poetry, write a good hand and converse elegantly. Entrance into court meant not only personal power, but also riches for the family. Hence the birth of a girl was as much welcomed as that of a boy. It is also interesting to note that the fine culture of the Tang period was bodily introduced into Japan by the Nipponese authorities of that period, and to this day the city of Kyoto, which for eleven centuries (until 1867) remained the imperial capital, still shows numerous reminiscences of ancient Chinese civilization, particularly in the coiffure, dress and ceremonies of the women.

The material for the present volume is gathered from one of the standard Chinese works, supplemented by historical facts from 中國歷史 , 通鑑輯覽 , 古今姓氏族譜 , 尚友錄 , 廿一史 , 韻府 , 唐詩 , as well as from valuable data obtained from the "Biography of Li Po" (李白) and from a poem by Po Chü-i (白居易) entitled "The Everlasting Wrong" (長恨歌).

Although there is a voluminous literature on Chinese bibliography, comparatively few books deal with women, far less the notable women of ancient times. Hence no apology is needed for presenting this study of the life of Yang Kuei-fei (楊貴妃). To translate accurately Chinese thoughts and ideas into a western language is difficult at any time, and the reader must excuse the quaint, though perhaps entertaining, phraseology used in some of the pages. But it is hoped that the very strangeness of a few of the scenes described many enhance the interest of the book and may even help the foreign reader to understand better certain aspects of Chinese culture and psychology, which seem to be at variance with what is generally found in the West.

In conclusion, I have to acknowledge much valuable assistance freely rendered to me by several friends, who wish to remain anonymous. Full acknowledgment is made in the footnotes of references to other authors.

THE AUTHOR.

55 Tung Tang Tze Hutung,
Peking, December 1st, 1923.

CONTENTS

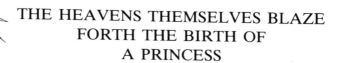

THE HEAVENS THEMSELVES BLAZE
FORTH THE BIRTH OF
A PRINCESS

EAUTY, grace and charm — these are the qualities that form the greatest attraction in a woman. Since the dawn of time, beauty has fed the fires of ambition. Wars have been waged; thrones have tottered; kingdoms have risen and waned — all because of the glorious charm of woman.

In the whole history of China, no beauty has been so universally praised as that of Yang Kuei-fei (楊貴妃), who was considered the loveliest woman of the Tang dynasty (A.D. 618-905).

Born at Hua-yin (華陰) in the district of T'ung-chou (同州) in Shensi (陝西) about two hundred li[1] east of the capital city of Chang-an (長安) (now Hsi-an 西安),

---

1. A li is one-third of an English mile.

1

Kuei-fei was the daughter of an official named Yang Hsuan-yen (楊玄琰), sometime President of the Board of War and holding the title of Duke under Emperor Jui-tsung (睿宗). Her personal name was Yu-huan (玉環), meaning "jade-circlet." Her parents were said to have experienced a strange vision on the night the child was born. They saw a brilliant meteor darting from the sky amidst magnificent rainbow lights which shone around their bed for some minutes, the meteor finally striking earth with a thunderous noise. The mother being superstitious, did not wish to rear her baby-girl, but the father insisted on keeping her. He thus reasoned with his wife: "When a girl is born with such a good omen, she is destined some day to become an empress; if not, she will at least attain to a very high position."

Kuei-fei was informed of this event as she grew up, and from childhood entertained the idea that she was no common person, but bound one day to be highly favoured at court.

Our heroine had three sisters, two elder and one younger, as well as a brother. The sisters were exceedingly pretty, but Kuei-fei surpassed them all. The father died when they were small children. The mother subsequently moved to the capital, where they lived with their paternal uncle, Yang Yuan-kuei (楊元珪). The uncle was ambitious and gave them the best education possible at home. He foresaw Kuei-fei's talent when she was young child, and likewise knew that she was born with a strange vision. He was therefore unusually partial to her and afforded her every advantage to further her ambitions. At the age of sixteen, Kuei-fei had mastered the Five Classics and Chinese history. Her exceptional alertness and activity of mind, combined with her unusual skill and love of music, enabled her to excel all three of her sisters. She took special interest in singing and in playing musical instruments, as well as in the art of dancing. She was adept in the composition of verses. Thus, she was well prepared for any high position which the future might have in store for her.

CHAPTER
TWO

MARRIAGE AS A STEPPING-STONE
TO AMBITION

HE beauty of Kuei-fei has often been compared to that of a lotus flower. Her dazzling loveliness was such that even if a little powder were applied to her face it would appear too white. On the other hand, the mere addition of a trace of carmine to her cheeks would render them too rosy. She was neither tall nor short, and any addition or diminution in this respect would have spoiled her rare features.

Her skin was as white in tint as the purest white jade and as soft to the touch as the softest silk. Her dreamy, amorous eyes, combined with her bewitching smile, sent a thrill of joy and desire through the most hard-hearted man. Above her olive-shaped eyes, the delicate brows curved like the arch of a swaying willow tree. Her mouth was small and well-shaped, while her teeth were set in two regular rows and of the colour of an unopened jasmine flower. It was said that in anger, as well as in delight, Kuei-fei's smiles scarcely ever left her. In fact, on one occasion, as we shall see later, even under the agonies of pain her sweet expression so fascinated the emperor Ming Huang that he gave in to all her whims and fancies.

Her bosom was exquisitely shaped, and both breasts were so natural and perfectly formed that the classical phrase, "Ming Huang adored Kuei-fei's breasts," exists to this day.

In fact, Kuei-fei was as faultlessly beautiful as any Chinese woman could be. Viewed casually from a distance, she might seem rather plump, but she was really of perfect build and proportion, that is, neither stout nor thin, and as agile as she was nimble, her whole contour being unspoilt by any artificial impediment, such as bound feet, tightened chest, and other deformities.

For years after her entry into the palace, a large number of court-maidens were especially set aside for preparing Kuei-fei's dresses, which were chosen and fashioned according to the flowers of the season. For the New Year (spring) she had blossoms of apricot, plum and narcissus; for summer, she adopted the lotus; for autumn, she patterned her gowns after the peony; for winter, she employed the chrysanthemum. Of jewellery she was fondest of pearls, and the finest gems of the world found their way into her boudoir and were frequently embroidered on her numerous dresses.

Kuei-fei was the embodiment of all that was lovely and extravagant. No wonder that no king, prince, courtier or humble attendant — who ever met her — could resist the allurement of her charms. Besides, she was the most artful of women and knew how to use her natural gifts to the best purpose. This unusual combination of beauty and artfulness she utilized to greater and greater advantage as she gained in experience. The emperor Ming Huang (明皇), supreme in the land and with thousands of the most handsome maidens to choose from, became a complete slave to her magnetic powers for twenty years, spending day and night in her company and giving up his whole kingdom for her sake. Even in the midst of national trouble and turmoil he clung steadily to her.

In A.D. 735, the emperor Ming Huang wanted to select a wife for his eighteenth son, Prince Shou (壽王). Kuei-fei's uncle heard the news and used every means, through the influence of a brother official, to spread the fame of her attractions, so that she might be chosen for the exalted position. This was eventually accomplished, much to the delight of the family. Kuei-fei was sixteen when she entered the palace. Her enchanting beauty fascinated the young prince. She proceeded at once to establish herself firmly in the good graces of her husband. By virtue of her charm, she soon became his favourite, and he wrote many poems in praise of her. Notwithstanding all the splendour of court life, Kuei-fei was discontented, for Prince Shou, though young and handsome, was not in the line of direct succession to the throne. Besides, our ambitious lady desired her name to be recorded in history as one of this world's greatest personages.

Chapter Three

CIRCUMSTANCES
BRINGING KUEI-FEI TO
THE EMPEROR

HREE years passed and spring had set in once
more. The imperial palace, with its high walls,
prominent towers and enclosed pavilions, looked
as grave and mighty as ever from the outside.
Within, the multitudinous courtyards were filled with
plants and flowers, while a crystal stream, spanned here
and there by marble bridges, meandered through spacious gardens. The cassia flowers were at their best and
lent much enchantment to the scene. The lakes were
surrounded by peach and pear trees in full bloom, and
roses of magnificent sizes and colours blossomed in all
their glory. White swans and ducks and fish of every
possible variety sported gaily in the water. Above, the
clear sky was invaded by the ceaseless singing of birds
and by the frolicky wind that whispered of spring air.

The roofs of the brilliantly painted colonnades were covered with wistaria, while straight poplars and curved weeping willows lined the sides.

Two parallel rows of red-lacquered pillars led to the crimson-coloured doors of His Majesty's private apartments. Through the open windows, shaded partly by neatly designed gauzework, was revealed the secluded royal chamber with its golden dragon-faced bedstead placed in the middle, while studded here and there at the sides were some couches decorated with gold lace and lacquer and inlaid with jade, pearls and other gems.

Hanging from the ceiling were silk-embroidered curtains set with pearls, corals, rubies and sapphires. Similar superbly designed swords, sceptres and screens were scattered in odd corners to represent the vast domains over which the reigning sovereign held sway.

Further on, along the inner halls and chambers, were displayed both green and white jade carvings of various designs and character in addition to large bronze tripods. Artificial trees of jade and coral set in delicate shaded pots, angular gold and jade wine-bowls, flower vases, curious snuff bottles, pretty ink-slabs of cornelian and topaz, as well as many other antique works of art were arrayed here and there. On the walls hung several pictures of palace scenes painted by the best court artists.

Groups of attentive maidens, dressed in rich, flowing robes, with long silken tassels hanging from their waists, and picturesque ornaments in their hair, sang rare songs and danced to the accompaniment of the choicest music.

Truly a scene complete and marvellous enough to satisfy the most fastidious! And yet the solitary occupant of the raised throne — Emperor Hsuan Tsung (玄宗), better known as Ming Huang (明皇) — was in a despondent mood. For several years he had reigned over a peaceful and prosperous empire. Successful wars had been waged and recalcitrant states subdued. During the intervals of peace, he had carried out several reforms enhancing the happiness of his subjects, Schools had been established in every village, and new industries had been founded. Literature and the arts had been encouraged in every direction. Even a college of music had been started for the first time in history, to which students of both sexes flocked. From the graduates of this institution he chose the most promising for the imperial presence and called them the "pear orchard" musicians. For some years he had given up his favourite game of polo to which he and his athletic military friends of younger days were much devoted. Thousands of the prettiest maidens from every corner of the Flowery Kingdom adorned the palace, but to few of these did His Majesty pay any attention. A calamity had suddenly overtaken the imperial household, for the emperor's favourite concubine had recently died after giving birth to a prince. Because of his passionate love for her, he had earlier banished the real Empress Wang and her own (and his) son, Crown Prince Ying (瑛太子), an action which the nation regretted. In came the chief eunuch and privy councillor, Kao Li-shih, who knew his monarch's desires and licentious habits, and suggested that an edict be promulgated ordering the officials to seek the prettiest girls in the kingdom, so that one might be chosen as imperial consort and the peace of mind of the Son of Heaven thereby restored. Kao himself traversed the entire country and after many weeks selected a beautiful and talented girl of sixteen years, later called Mei-fei (梅妃), from the city of Hsing-hua (興化) in Fukien province. This favoured one was brought to the palace and presented to the emperor. He was much pleased with her, for the bride was not only pretty but likewise gifted in music, poetry and other accomplishments. But her modest and quiet disposition did not long satisfy the emperor's lascivious and ever-changing tastes. Nevertheless, Mei-fei's beauty ranked first among the three thousand maidens in the palace. She was the newest favourite and the emperor loved her dearly. Officials from all parts of China sent plum trees as tribute to the court, for Mei-fei liked their blossoms above all others. Thus, the whole palace soon assumed the aspect of a magnificent bower of the choicest white blossoms.

One night, the emperor gave a garden-party to the princes and courtiers, and commanded Mei-fei to dance. In the midst of one of her elegant poses, a passing knight, perhaps somewhat tipsy, accidentally stepped on her shoes. She at once asked to be excused and retired to her own apartments furious over the incident. The unhappy courtier spent the whole night lamenting his fate. He attended court early next morning, threw himself at the emperor's feet and begged His Majesty to end his unworthy existence. The latter, however, was of a benevolent disposition and smiled at his disconsolate subject, saying: "How can I let you suffer notwithstanding the esteem in which I hold my beautiful queen? The affair being unpremeditated, I will overlook it."

But the mind of the courtier was still disturbed for fear that Mei-fei might not entirely forgive him. He therefore consulted a friend, also an official, who was full of schemes and in whom the emperor had much faith. This second courtier approached the sovereign one day, saying:"There are over three thousand court-maidens. Why should Your Majesty not choose one for consort?" The emperor sighed. "Though I have waited, I have not yet met the most suitable mate in the world with whom I can enjoy everlasting happiness. Oh, how I long for one who is so ravishing that she may even upset an empire, such as I have read about in history! Then shall I be truly contented." To this extravagant outburst the schemer replied: "Has Your Majesty not heard of Prince Shou's favourite? I am told her beauty is incomparable." The emperor at once lost his *ennui* and ordered the head eunuch to proceed to Prince Shou's palace and bring Kuei-fei immediately to him. On hearing the summons, Kuei-fei was much perturbed, not knowing what fate awaited her. With mingled joy and sorrow, she went in tears to bid farewell to Prince Shou, saying:"Your humble wife had hoped that we might always enjoy our lives together. Who could have thought that the emperor would send for me to-day? I fear after this separation we may never meet again."

The prince held her hands tenderly and wept aloud, saying:"Just as the flower is blooming, the wind smites it. Just as the moon is full, the clouds veil it. From earliest times until now, misfortunes ever cross the path of life. Under the present circumstances, there is nothing to do but obey the emperor's command. If you do not meet with his favour, we may yet see each other again. My beloved, do take care of yourself and thus comfort my sorely tried heart." The eunuch became impatient and told them to make haste, as the Son of Heaven was waiting.

Accompanied by an imperial escort, Kuei-fei was conveyed to the palace and ushered at dusk into the presence of His Majesty. The whole palace was illuminated with lanterns. Bright moon-beams streamed into every corner of the audience hall, revealing all the more Kuei-fei's unrivalled beauty. The emperor cast one long glance at this fairest of women. Her sparkling and graceful movement fascinated every onlooker and captivated His Majesty's heart. He had never before beheld a face so exquisite in its contour or freshness, for it was without spot or blemish, nor had he ever seen a more enchanting figure in his whole life. No wonder the fate of an empire could be overturned by her! The emperor at once became enamoured of her. He hesitated awhile, doubting whether it would be proper for him to claim her right away, for even a Son of Heaven feared criticism from outside. The confidential eunuch therefore suggested that His Majesty should command Prince Shou to marry the daughter of a marshal and that Kuei-fei herself should appeal to her husband in her own name to be allowed to live as a nun on probation. This scheme was duly carried out, and Kuei-fei retired temporarily as a nun to the T'ai-chen Palace, where she received the rank of T'ai-chen Fei (太眞妃).

It was only natural that after this incident there should be a wide-spread feeling of uneasiness and a number of amusing rumours. The emperor secretly sought Kuei-fei's presence daily. She, on her part, used every wit, charm and her growing influence with the Son of Heaven to secure her appointment as imperial consort. Eventually, the emperor became so infatuated with her that he spent the night in her company. Kuei-fei shed graceful tears, which the emperor wiped away with his own handkerchief. When he asked for the reason, she replied:"I am like a flower just in bloom. My lord loves me now, but will he still remember me when my beauty fades? Pray give me a pledge that thou wilt love me always." The emperor was deeply touched by these words. He seized from the table a pair of bracelets and two gold pins shaped like phoenixes and set in pearls, and gave one of each kind to Kuei-fei as tokens of his undying love, saying: "Dearest, in all my six palaces the thousands of maidens living therein are as dust compared with thee. For years I have been waiting for such a love as thine, and even if I were to spend night and day without interruption with thee, these succeeding years would not make up for the loss of past bliss that might have been mine. How could I, therefore ever change toward thee, my best beloved? If I should ever be unfaithful to thee, may Heaven strike me down and destroy my kingdom."

On hearing these memorable words, Kuei-fei immediately knelt down and thanked His Majesty for the promise.

"Be of good cheer, my dearest one," continued the emperor, "to-morrow thou shalt receive thy title of Kuei-fei[1] and be openly received at court. We will then enjoy everlasting happiness together."

---

1. *Kuei-fei* is a title signifying "imperial concubine" and not her maiden name.

*CHAPTER
FOUR*

HER CALL TO THE PALACE

HE next day a full court assembled at Phoenix Hall with every possible pomp and grandeur to welcome Kuei-fei to the palace. Her uncle, her brother and her cousin Yang Kuo-chung were raised to high ranks, and her three sisters also received titles of nobility, besides numerous presents and thousands of gold pieces. This news was circulated throughout the country, and many parents of that time prayed that they might have pretty daughters rather than sons. Every day after audience the imperial lover visited Kuei-fei, who used every means to win his heart. At one moment she would sing "The Rainbow Skirt and Feather Jacket," composed by herself, and enthral him. At another, she would purposely scatter her jewellery and pieces of clothing on the floor in order that he might himself gather them up and help her to

16

dress. In fact, the artful woman succeeded in fascinating the emperor to such an extent that he began to neglect his regal duties to the nation. Her influence soon became paramount and her position as the all-powerful favourite was completely assured hereafter.

For a fortnight, the emperor had entirely forgotten Mei-fei, the senior imperial concubine. She wondered what could have prevented him from visiting her, as he had never before allowed three days to pass without seeing her. She became impatient and sent for the head eunuch, who fell on his knees and observed: "Your humble servant has heard that His Majesty has taken over the concubine of Prince Shou. The imperial master's face is beaming with joy these days."

At this, Mei-fei could not restrain her tears and wept bitterly. The maids-in-waiting tried their best to console her, and one of them suggested that Mei-fei should attire herself in her loveliest dress and seek the emperor in person. Weary at heart, she faced the mirror and cried aloud: "Oh, Heaven, why shouldst thou be so cruel to me? Am I not as lovely and clever as that other woman? Why should such a sad fate befall a life as young as mine?"

Her feelings at this period may best be described in the following verse:

"Than colours of the peony my raiment is more fair,
  The breeze across the palace lake takes fragrance from my hair,
  My love is hidden in my breast, a fan conceals my pain,
  A clear moon in an autumn night, I wait my lord in vain."

At the end of an hour, she dressed in her best clothes and walked slowly towards the emperor's private grounds. She came upon His Majesty as he was strolling in the garden. The emperor looked surprised and asked, "What good wind has blown my beloved here?" Mei-fei replied, in a low tone: "The spring air is exhilarating, the flowers are in full bloom, the birds are singing, and my heart being lonesome, I thought of taking a walk. I hear Your Majesty has a new bride and I have come purposely to offer my humble congratulations." The emperor answered: "Such pleasure is only for the time being. I do hope my sweet beloved will not be disturbed."

Chapter five

MEETING OF TWO BEAUTIES

AS Mei-fei insisted upon meeting Kuei-fei, the emperor agreed to send for the latter, provided Mei-fei would control her feelings. Matters having been arranged, Kuei-fei arrived in her stately way and knelt before her senior, saying: "Long live the empress. Thy unworthy slave herewith prostrates herself."

The emperor ordered wine to be served in honour of the occasion. But the meeting, instead of smoothing matters over, rapidly increased the jealousy and hatred on both sides. His Majesty was more attracted by the sprightly wit and delightful humour of the beautiful, domineering Kuei-fei than by the delicate, quieter and more orthodox charm of Mei-fei. The former was surpassingly lovely. She was specially noted as being the only plump one among China's historical beauties. The days of the gentle, scrupulous, composed Mei-fei were destined to end, and in her place someone more coquettish, more crafty and determined had stepped in. She felt herself confronted by a personality as proud as, and probably prouder than, her own.

While they were drinking wine, each pretended to write a poem in praise of the other's fine qualities. For instance, Mei-fei composed a fine seven-character poem of four verses, apparently extolling her rival's accomplishments, but really slighting her by comparing her face to the full moon. Translated roughly, the poem reads:

"Like the Wu peak embracing clouds of Ch'u,[1]
  Like fairies of Jade Pavilion His Majesty is ever feasting with
        thee;
  Who could approach thy face so fair and full as the moon.
  Half the monarch's flowery land sacrified through thee!"

To this, Kuei-fei retorted in a poem, also of seven characters in each line, of perhaps less poignancy:

"Through many winters thy beauty remains unchanged,
  Like the plum blossom snow-white and unchallenged,
  Thou hast inhaled the spring air rather too early,
  How can common flowers like me compare with thee?"[2]

---

1. The first line is a famous quotation comparing the embrace of two lovers to that of a famous mountain in Szechwan province with its ever-topping clouds.
2. "Mei," the first name of Mei-fei, means plum, whose flowers are white. Her rival tried to hint that, because Mei-fei had entered the palace earlier, her beauty and attractions were passing away.

The emperor treated them with impartial courtesy and complimented each upon her unique talent in arts and literature. He was pleased that both appeared on terms of courtesy and amiability. Nevertheless, before many months had passed, Kuei-fei, through schemes and artifices so dear and natural to women when the other sex is lost in admiration, had become so powerful that she succeeded in getting her rival removed to a lonely part of the east palace, where the broken-hearted woman was doomed to spend the rest of her life in solitude. How bitter must have been her thoughts to be thus a victim of the other's trickery and machinations!

CHAPTER
SIX

THE ETERNAL TRIANGLE

ONE day, while she was lamenting her fate, Mei-fei received a verbal message from the head eunuch, who said, "His Majesty has sent for Her Highness to visit him at the palace, but does not wish Kuei-fei to know." On hearing this, she became agitated and asked him: "The Son of Heaven has supreme power. Life and death are in his hands. Why should His Majesty be afraid of that insignificant fat slave?"

Nevertheless, she dressed in her most becoming clothes and was soon mounted on her white pony on the way to the emperor's chamber. On reaching his presence, she knelt down and broke out in sobs: "Your humble wife thought that she had been entirely forsaken. She never dared dream of seeing Your Majesty again." The emperor stretched out his hands, and, lifting her up, said affectionately: "Have I not been thinking of thee every day, my dear one? I notice thou art looking thinner these days."

Mei-fei replied, "Under such sad circumstances, is it strange that I should look pale and not as well as the fat one does?" His Majesty avoided a direct answer and observed diplomatically: "Come, come, do not be down-hearted. Each of you has your unique qualities." As usual, wine was brought in, and they spent the evening together. The loving monarch poured out soothing and passionate words, which gradually calmed Mei-fei's tumultuous heart and foreboding spirit, and reminded her of the heavenly delight of that first moment when she entered the palace. Alas, it now seemed ages ago! Her natural sweetness and uncomplaining devotion to her imperial master once more asserted themselves as in the olden days.

Meanwhile, Kuei-fei, in her own apartments, waited in vain for the emperor's morning visit. She asked an attendant and was told that her lord had spent the night with Mei-fei at Pei-hua Palace. Swiftly she made her way thither and entered His Majesty's bed-chamber without any formality.

"Your Majesty is late to-day in giving audience to the waiting ministers" she rudely exclaimed. "No, my love," retorted the emperor, assuming a level voice, though his mind was really very ill at ease, "it is you who are too early." Hastily, he drew the curtains together and concealed his other love behind them. Kuei-fei had, however, noticed a pair of embroidered slippers underneath the bed, as well as jade hairpins and bracelets by the pillow, so inquired angrily: "Who has been spending the happy night with Your Majesty, that you do not even know it is now daylight? Your Majesty ought to be in the throne room attending to state affairs. I will wait here until my lord is ready." The emperor was ashamed and pleaded that he was unwell and so could not hold audience. At this, Kuei-fei burst into a fit of uncontrolled passion. She threw all her ornaments on the floor and returned directly to her secluded quarters in the west palace.

In the meantime, one of the eunuchs, fearing that Kuei-fei might attempt some other mischievous act, accompanied the passive Mei-fei back to her chamber. After the excitement had subsided, and on discovering that Mei-fei had left, the emperor became angry, as he desired to spend more time with her. He himself gathered Kuei-fei's discarded ornaments and sent them over to Mei-fei instead. On receiving these, she wrote the following pathetic verse:

"I no longer paint my eye-brows or ornament my hair,
 My clothes are wet with my falling tears.
 In my lonely dwelling, I need no jewellery
 To comfort my weary hours."

The emperor, after reading the poem, heaved a deep sigh and murmured to himself: "Woe is me! Lives there a woman in this world who is not jealous of another?"

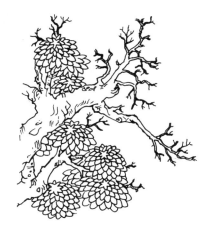

CHAPTER
SEVEN

KUEI-FEI'S RUSES
AND FANCIES

NE day Mei-fei overheard that the governor of Kwantung province had sent a handsome tribute to the court. She asked of her servants if there were plum blossoms for her, as she loved them so. The head eunuch answered, "No, they are fresh *lichi*[1] sent as a gift to Her Highness Kuei-fei."

Mei-fei then inquired in a voice of constraint: "You are a constant attendant upon His Majesty. Do you think he still remembers my name?" To this the eunuch replied, "His Majesty is as fond of Your Highness as ever, but he greatly fears Kuei-fei's jealousy." Upon hearing this she exclaimed: "I hear that, in the olden days when Empress Chen was deserted by

---

1. Cantonese juicy fruit with loose scaly shell, oval stone and sweetly flavoured pulp.

25

Emperor Wu in the Han dynasty, she paid a well-known poet thousands of silver pieces to write a touching poem for presentation to her lord. The sovereign was deeply moved, recalled her to the palace and thereafter they were again united until the end. If there is any way of procuring for me a poet as wise as that one, I am willing to pay anything within my power."

But the eunuch was afraid of Kuei-fei's displeasure and had not the courage to suggest any name. He replied instead: "Her Highness is very able; why not compose a poem herself? This will appeal more strongly to the emperor."

Mei-fei thought the matter over, then took up her brush with shaking hands, but for some moments was unable to compose a line. Her anguish was like a sharp sword piercing her heart. Finally, by dint of perseverance and after many searchings of her soul, she finished a long poem, describing her loneliness and praying for the emperor's companionship. The power of her pen was marvellously revealed in this writing. On receiving the fine composition, the monarch read it with tearful eyes. His conscience was deeply smitten and he uttered a moan of unspeakable pain and sympathy. Kuei-fei, ever at his side nowadays, perceived this with her usual jealousy and spoke in a reproachful tone to him: "Mei-fei is only a common woman. How dare she complain of being lonely? She deserves to be killed." His Majesty remained silent, but she repeatedly brought up the subject. Eventually, he burst out: "Poor Mei-fei is all alone. Her poem contains nothing impure. How can I expect my people to be contented and peaceful if I kill an innocent soul like hers?" Kuei-fei retorted in a sarcastic tone, "Well, since Your Majesty cannot dismiss your fond memory of her, why not again seek for a happy reunion at Pei-hua Palace?"[1] But the distracted monarch, knowing well her jealous nature and wishing to avoid at all cost a repetition of that disgraceful scene, compromised by saying: "Let not such a small affair interfere with your state of mind, my love. Do refrain from bringing the matter up again."

Kuei-fei had a special liking for fresh *lichi*. To gratify her wishes the emperor dispatched fast mounted guards to fetch the best kinds, and an imperial edict was issued authorizing the officials en route to provide relays of swift horses for these guards, so that they might ccomplete the return journey in five days.[2] Failure to accomplish the task within the specified time meant corporal punishment to the guards and degradation in rank to the civil officials concerned. Needless to say, such arbitrary laws for such a ludicrous purpose produced consternation among the people and did not enhance the popularity of the favourite.

Consider the amount of energy and money wasted

---

1. This refers to the sorry incident in the preceding chapter.
2. Total distance as the crow flies from Canton to Chang-an (Hsi-an), six hundred English miles.

merely for the selfish and temporary gratification of one idle woman's fancies! Even the masses expressed their disapproval. Is it any wonder that the country was gradually brought to ruin through the emperor's seeking to meet Kuei-fei's numberless extravagant requirements, and neglecting real state burdens as well as the crying needs of his subjects?

Chapter eight

JADE-FISH AS A SPECIFIC FOR TOOTHACHE

A S the years rolled on, Kuei-fei grew more and more jealous of Mei-fei. Realizing that she could not induce the emperor to kill her rival, she kept brooding over the matter and filled the palace with an unpleasant atmosphere. Whenever anger got the better of her, she invariably developed a toothache, varying in intensity according to whether or not her desires were granted. At such times, she would refuse to talk or eat, far less to cast her bewitching smile around. When referring to Mei-fei before the emperor, she would sometimes resort to irony and sarcasm, hoping thereby to attain her object. The emperor was always full of apologies and in endearing terms would

29

gently pat her on the cheek or lightly pinch her faultless skin, and ask her to overlook the past.

On one occasion, the emperor saw Kuei-fei resting her flushed face with knitted brows on one hand, and apparently suffering from a troublesome toothache. He rushed up to her, and stroking her cheek exclaimed, "How I wish the pain might fall upon me instead of my sweet one!" On receiving no response, His Majesty was worried and issued instructions to the imperial physicians to discover without delay the best remedy for Her Highness' malady. One of the courtiers submitted that belonging to a certain rich family, named Chu, there was a mysterious kind of fish, called *jade-fish*, which possessed the property of quenching thirst as well as stopping toothache. The emperor immediately ordered this to be brought post-haste to the palace. After one application of this wonderful remedy to the aching spot, the suffering beauty obtained instant relief, due no doubt to its soothing action. His Majesty was exceedingly pleased with the result and rewarded the lucky adviser with twenty pounds of gold, three thousand loads of rice and thirty rolls of cloth. Henceforth, he did not dare to vex his favourite again for fear the slightest annoyance might bring about a recurrence of the dreaded pain. Thus, her anger and complaint, real or imaginary, were a means of furthering her power and influence over the emperor. Her revengeful temperament also contributed to her being more and more feared in the palace. The monarch's infatuation and limitless patience with Kuei-fei proved to be his greatest folly, bringing ruin, not only upon himself, but also in the end upon his whole empire.

CHAPTER
NINE

THE GARDEN BANQUET AND
ITS SEQUEL

N one occasion, the emperor invited several princes and courtiers to an evening party. The guests asked to be granted an interview with Kuei-fei, to which His Majesty graciously consented. Accordingly, he led his beautiful spouse to a raised seat in the garden. When the banquet was over, and the guests had departed, Kuei-fei seized a flute belonging to Prince Ning and played it for a while. The emperor jokingly said to her, "Why don't you blow your own flute, as Prince Ning has just used that one, and it is still warm with his breath?"

Kuei-fei's face turned red, as she slowly but deliberately put the instrument aside and answered: "What harm can there be in blowing a flute previously used by another? I have been told that a certain person's shoes were once stepped upon, and yet Your Majesty did not mind it.[1] Why then reprove your humble wife for using the flute?"

The emperor became enraged. For months he had already been displeased with her constant bickerings over Mei-fei. Instead of offering thanks to him for the evening's grand entertainment, she showed her temper over a jest about which he was not serious. Her unreasonable complaint roused the wrath of the sovereign to such a pitch that he scolded her in a loud tone: "Yu-huan,[2] how dare you behave so rudely before me? You have indeed gone too far." He at once commanded the chief eunuch to send her back without delay to her parents' home at Hua-yin and forbade her to wait upon him again. Kuei-fei felt as if a thunder bolt had struck her unawares. Her whole frame quivered under the shock, and she broke down in bitter tears. There appeared now no loophole for escape; her ambition was thwarted and her career ended. The once powerful favourite was unable to save her own position, seeing nothing before her but the decline of influence and the dwindling of her peace and happiness.

Filled with shame and remorse, she prepared to journey to her parent's home, accompanied by her personal eunuch. Sorrowfully she bade him gather all

---

1. See Chapter III.
2. Kuei-fei's maiden name.

her treasures and belongings and dispatch them after her. The rustling of the wind, as it moaned fretfully through the trees along the way, seemed to echo her sad thoughts. Sobs choked her further utterance until relief came in a surging flood of tears. When she burst through the door of her home her relatives stood there in utter dismay, knowing not what to make of this unlooked-for disaster. The mother noticed that her poor daughter was in a deplorable condition — a forlorn, forsaken, and dejected being. She had been the sole pride of the family, and in her all their high hopes had centred. Now these expectations were suddenly shattered, like fragile porcelain, and their grief and disappointment were beyond words.

This period of temporary exile has been immortalized in verse by two poets of the time.

The first, Li Po, thus describes the event:

"Before my hall sweet flowers perfume the calm and silent night.
I wish to roll the blinds — but, ah! am checked by Spring's despite.
Dimly, guitar beneath my arm, the glancing moon I see.
The wavering colours of the trees obscure my lost delight."[1]

The second poet, Li Yi, composed the following poem:

"With freshened dew the flowers are damp in Springtide's fragrant bowers.

---

1. Translated by W. J. B. Fletcher.

In Chao-yang Court[1] the sound of songs disturbs the moon lit
        hours.
As slow as if it held the sea drips on the water clock.
Its tedious dripping seems to me the long-drawn night to mock."[2]

---

1. Residence of the empress when out of favour.
2. Translated by W. J. B. Fletcher.

CHAPTER
TEN

RECALLED TO
CREATER GLORY

I N the meantime, the emperor was acutely distressed, and try as he would, he could find no solace from any of the thousands and more of court-maidens around him. He missed Kuei-fei's presence most keenly. The loneliness was more than he could bear. For several days he was indisposed. He seriously considered the recall of his earlier love, the neglected Mei-fei, but was informed that Kuei-fei contemplated her assassination, so this plan had to be abandoned. The palace attendants witnessed frequent torrential outbursts of rage from the Son of Heaven. Every one, from the highest courtier to the lowliest eunuch and maid attendant, suffered His Majesty's displeasure, and often undeserved punishment for the slightest offence. Nothing seemed capable of pleasing the emperor, and it appeared as if consolation were only possible if the disgraced favourite were brought back to his side. The whole world seemed desolate and meaningless, for the separation had intensified the emperor's moments of enforced solitude.

The head eunuch, ever anticipating his master's true needs, skilfully contrived with Yang Kuo-chung to restore the latter's cousin, Kuei-fei, to power. With that end in view Kuo-chung urged a certain courtier to find means to effect a reconciliation between the two lovers. Consequently, this wily official at an early audience greeted the emperor with the following words: "May it please Your Majesty! Her Highness Kuei-fei, whose beauty and charm excel anything the princesses and fair maidens in the six palaces can lay claim to, has committed a grave crime and deserves to die. Nevertheless, she should do so within a small place inside the palace grounds. Why disgrace her by allowing her to die outside?"

The disconsolate ruler could not suppress his grief on hearing this. He forthwith left the audience hall and gave orders for the chief eunuch to prepare many costly presents to be sent to his fallen consort.

When the messenger arrived, Kuei-fei's heart leapt with joy, though mingled with uncertainty. In those weeks of disgrace, life had indeed been a misery to her, and this sudden news was almost too good to be true. Even now, her artfulness came to the fore. Amid tears she said to the eunuch: "I have sinned and deserve to die, but have now received forgiveness from my illustrious lord. To-day my sovereign commands me to return to my former position. How can I face the world? Shall I not be jeered at? There is nothing I possess that has not come from my beloved sovereign, except my miserable life, which my parents gave me. Under such circumstances, I regret having nothing worthy to present to His Majesty except this small lock of hair, which please take back to my lord as a token of my undying love and gratitude. You can tell the emperor that I am about to kill myself and beg him not to worry any more about me."

The eunuch was frightened and immediately conveyed to the waiting sovereign the serious news, together with the token of her farewell. His Majesty was overwhelmed with remorse and issued orders at once for some trusted messengers to start at midnight and fetch Kuei-fei back to the palace in the fragrant chariot.[1] On their arrival at her mansion, she felt that the tide of fortune had indeed turned and that Heaven's favour once more smiled upon her. She undertook the journey of two hundred li without delay, and permitted her mind to dwell upon former luxuries and future pleasures. She was dressed in a simple, fawn-coloured gown, and, when she arrived at the palace, proceeded directly to the emperor, kneeling before him in silent entreaty, broken only by half-smothered sobs. The

---

1. Made of sandal wood.

monarch gently lifted her up. Tears of supremest joy flowed from the eyes of both lovers. He whispered words of tender love and devotion to his beloved and ordered the maids-in-waiting to clothe her in the finest imperial robes. Hand in hand, trembling still under the torments of the long days which had separated them, they became once more enraptured by the thrill of their reunion. Thus, they spent a joyous evening, renewing their former affection.

On the following morning, the palace was agog with excitement, and banquets were once more the order of the day. All the imperial clans assembled to congratulate Kuei-fei on her restoration to fame and glory. Henceforth, the emperor lavished his love unstintedly upon the returned favourite, and gave himself up entirely to a life of reckless orgy and dissipation.

A FOSTER SON

A T this time a youth of Tartar descent, named An Lu-shan, of noble bearing but of a crafty and daring disposition, was introduced to the court. The emperor took a great fancy to him and thought that he was an honest simpleton. An Lu-shan soon gained the full confidence of the monarch, who showed great partiality towards him and permitted him unusual liberties in the privacy of the palace.

One day he brought a pretty white parrot with red legs in a golden cage and presented it to the emperor. He pretended to be ignorant of etiquette by kneeling only before the emperor and not before the heir apparent. On the emperor's asking, "Why don't you salute the prince?" An Lu-shan replied, "Your humble subject knows not what a prince's title is; how dare he therefore pay the same homage to the prince in the presence of the Supreme Ruler?"

The emperor said again, "The Heir Apparent is the Son of Heaven. Some day when I mount the dragon, he will succeed to the throne and rule the empire."

An Lu-shan quickly apologized and made obeisance to the prince and exclaimed: "I only knew that I must worship and serve the emperor with entire devotion, and had no idea His Highness was entitled to the same honour. Pray forgive this ignorant servant." The emperor turned to the prince and said, "I like this simple-minded lad; he seems very frank."

While the emperor and prince were talking, a group of court-maidens, escorting Kuei-fei in her fragrant chariot, arrived. Pointing to An Lu-shan, she asked, "Who is that man and what is his rank?" The monarch replied: "He is an official in Fan-yang, a man of Tartar descent. I am keeping him to serve me in the court. He is a foster-son of Chang Shou-k'uei (張守珪), and as he is staying with me, I look upon him as my own foster-son as well."

"He looks indeed a fine lad," said Kuei-fei, to which the emperor replied, "If you regard him in the same way, then we will keep him as our joint foster-son."

An Lu-shan had long ago heard of the famous beauty, and now seized this opportunity to win her approval by kneeling down and addressing her thus: "Long live my foster-mother and great empress!" Kuei-fei felt flattered and did not conceal her unusual liking for him. She cast upon him her amorous eyes and bewitching smile to reciprocate his attentions.

"You ought to make obeisance to the father first and then the mother," said the emperor to An Lu-shan, to which the latter responded, "But forgive my stupidity, Your Majesty; it is our Tartar custom to pay respect first to the mother." The emperor smiled and said to Kuei-fei, "Isn't he dense?"

One day, when An Lu-shan was leaning on a chair opposite to that occupied by the emperor, the Son of Heaven addressed him thus: "I wonder what is inside your big stomach?" An Lu-shan craftily replied, "There is nothing inside but my loyal devotion to Your Majesty." The emperor was highly pleased with this flattery and trusted him more fully than ever. All the time the monarch was not aware of An Lu-shan's treachery and hypocrisy. Since their first meeting, Kuei-fei and the young Tartar had been attracted to each other. Mutual lust and admiration developed. As the days passed, the man's infatuation for his imperial mistress increased. This fact excited much attention and gossip in the palace, as well as the outside world. The sovereign, being now reduced to a weak debauchee, noticed nothing, as his entire mind was centred blindly upon his faithless spouse.

Their natures henceforth met only in that fusion of pleasure and abandon wherewith love itself could lend even tragedy and pain to its own use.

AN INDISCREET SCENE

WHEN An Lu-shan's birthday came, the emperor, Kuei-fei and all her relatives celebrated the occasion elaborately for three days. At the end of the festivities, An Lu-shan arrived to offer thanks to his foster-parents. He asked for permission to visit his foster-mother to which the emperor replied: "She has just retired, after having spent half a day in entertaining. You may go and seek her yourself."

Kuei-fei was in a reclining and half-intoxicated condition[1] when An Lu-shan entered. Her cheeks were rose-coloured, while her soft dreamy eyes were partially closed. She looked exceedingly beautiful, enchanting and desirable. On noticing him, Kuei-fei said

---

1. Kuei-fei was very fond of the winecup. One of the greatest plays on the Chinese stage is "Kuei-fei Intoxicated."

lazily: "My foster-son, it is the custom for a new-born babe to have a bath three days after its birth. Your birthday is just over and you should observe the same custom." So saying, she ordered the attendants to seize him, remove his outer gown and wrap his body with a silk quilt. He was then placed in a chariot and wheeled about in the courtyard, as if they were proceeding to give him a bath, in the same way that they would any ordinary baby. This scene created much laughter. The noise aroused the attention of the emperor, who was reading in the garden beyond. His Majesty made haste to see what was happening. When he saw the joke, he too enjoyed the lively scene and presented twenty thousand taels of silver to An Lu-shan as a bath present.

One beautiful spring afternoon, while a cool wind was blowing and the air was filled with the fragrance of myriads of flowers, the emperor and An Lu-shan were admiring the spring prospect from the palace hall. The former looked round for Kuei-fei, but she was not to be seen. He sent word for her to come out in her ordinary dress. She had just finished her bath and looked unusually charming in her loose-flowing garments. This attracted the emperor's attention, and he remarked, "You look exceedingly pretty, my beloved."

At this moment, a lacquered case containing some foreign perfumes arrived and was placed before His Majesty. The emperor asked Kuei-fei to face the polished bronze mirror while he himself sprinkled a few drops of the contents over her face. He brought a chair, sat next to her and applied the remaining perfume to her half-bare shoulders. Accidentally the large sleeves dropped down exposing her beautiful coral-tinted breasts. The emperor exclaimed, "Oh! how lovely, how exquisite!"[1]

An Lu-shan, who was standing near by, inadvertently remarked, "Yes, as smooth and delicate to the touch as satin!"

The secret was out! All save the emperor stood still, aghast and speechless. What if His Majesty should suspect the improper relation between Kuei-fei and An Lu-shan!

No wonder Kuei-fei was greatly alarmed. She trembled from head to foot for fear that the emperor would find out about their secret intimacy. Maids and eunuchs held their breath, staring at one another in the utmost fright. But the fond emperor was not a bit suspicious. He asked smilingly, "My Tartar lad, you dull boy, how do you know that they are so smooth and delicate as satin?"

This incident showed how completely the imperial lover was under the spell of Kuei-fei's hypnotic influence. He merely concentrated his attention upon the extraordinarily attractive, living idol before him and laughed merrily. Kuei-fei and the attendants thereupon

---

1. "Ming Huang adored Kuei-fei's breasts" is a popular saying handed down from that time.

45

followed with louder peals of laughter in order to save this most embarrassing situation.

It is recorded that every one at court knew of An Lu-shan's illicit relations with Kuei-fei. Many whispers were heard inside the celestial palace, high and low expressing their wonder at An Lu-shan's daring so publicly to express his improper love for the imperial concubine. As An Lu-shan grew in years and in favour with Kuei-fei, so also his arrogance increased. His conceit soon knew no bounds and this made enemies.

Kuei-fei's cousin, Yang Kuo-chung (楊國忠), a powerful minister at court, entertained an intense hatred for An Lu-shan. He madly loved Kuei-fei's youngest sister, but she preferred the company of the handsome An Lu-shan. Kuo-chung therefore plotted to get rid of his rival by expelling him from the capital. The latter, realizing his perilous situation, prepared an application for temporary retirement. At a morning audience Kuo-chung submitted the following plan to the emperor: "Ho-tung is a strategic fortress. As An Lu-shan is the only general competent to take charge of that city, may I suggest his being sent there?" The emperor agreed, and summoning An Lu-shan to him, said: "You have served me faithfully. I ought to keep you near me, but Ho-tung is a very important place and the savage tribes are now troublesome. I want you to go and do your best to maintain peace there for me." The emperor then appointed him military governor of three frontier cities — Ping-lu (平盧), Fan-yang (范陽) and

Ho-tung (河東), all lying along the northern borders of the present Chihli and Shansi provinces. This meant that he had the best and largest armies of the empire under his immediate command. An Lu-shan thanked the sovereign and made the necessary preparation for his journey. Kuei-fei secretly invited her lover to come to her private chamber. she held his hands for a long time, and tearfully said: "Your leaving the palace is entirely due to my cousin Kuo-chung's jealous disposition. We have spent many happy hours together in the most secluded corners of the palace. How can I bear to be separated from you now? Who will compensate me for the tears of sorrow at our parting? Rest assured that I will use every means, by diplomacy or otherwise, to influence the emperor and recall you to court."

These fond words gave much comfort to her lover. An Lu-shan took his departure with great reluctance. This humiliating treatment by Yang Kuo-chung exasperated him, and the more he reflected the more angry he became. Eventually he vowed that he would one day seek revenge upon his enemy. He, therefore, sowed seeds of dissension throughout the land, which took deep root. Little dreaming to what depths of folly this personal hatred might lead him, he played a desperate game to betray the sovereign who trusted him and jeopardize the security of the state he was supposed to serve.

In the meantime, Kuei-fei, yearning for her young lover, lost her usual appetite and sleep and became greatly depressed. The emperor, not suspecting the true reason, and thinking only of his pleasures, sought to please his concubine in every possible way. Secure thus in the increasing love and blind devotion of her infatuated sovereign, she kept him practically under her thumb, he being a mere puppet in her hands! No wonder the strength and prestige of the country steadily declined, principally because of the remarkable fascination exercised by one unusual woman upon the absolute ruler of the land.

ENCOUNTER WITH THE
GREAT POET LI PO

NE bright October day a large collection of peony flowers in different varieties and colours was received as a tribute from the south. The emperor and his favourite were admiring these exquisite blooms, when Kuei-fei exclaimed, "These fragrant flowers are indeed pleasing to Your Majesty's eyes." The emperor replied, "Fragrant indeed are these flowers, but my darling is above all the queen of loving flowers."

Soon afterwards, there came a group of sixteen young "pear orchard" musicians, each holding an instrument. At their head was the well-known player Li Kuei-nien (李龜年). The emperor said, "Kuei-fei is wearing a new robe to-day, so the old verses are not appropriate for the occasion." Accordingly he sent Li

Keui-nien on horseback to fetch the leading poet of the day, Li Po (李白), in order that some special verses might be composed for the occasion. Li Po (A.D. 705–762) was a man of exceptional intellect and lofty motives. Best of all he loved to write about the beautiful scenery which surrounded him at youth. He wandered far and wide in the country with five other similarly minded individuals. For some time these six wanderers of the "Bamboo Grove" drank and wrote verses to their hearts' content, and then they retired to the mountains. By and by, Li Po's fame reached the capital. To this day, Li Po ranks first among China's poets and his works have seen hundreds of editions.

After some hours of search, Li Kuei-nien found the great scholar in one of the wine shops in Chang-an Street and took him to the palace. It was only after having had his body wrapped in blankets and his face mopped with cold water that Li Po woke up and was then introduced to the emperor as a "banished angel." The emperor received him with marked favour, himself offered Li Po some refreshing soup and commanded Kuei-fei to hold the ink-slab while the great man was putting his thoughts into immortal words. Realizing that the most dazzling beauty of the court was conferring upon him an unprecedented honour, he dashed off some of his most eloquent and impassioned lines.

"Mid happy flowers the loveliest still his favourite's beauty rare:
This Breath of Balm to dissipate what boundless hate arose!
The well-remembered arbour floods his heart with scented care.

Upon the clouds I gaze and see thy vesture floating fair.
Upon the flowers I gaze and lo! thy cheek is kindling there.
The zephyr brushing through the stoep thy footfall seems to be.
The dew, so like thy freshness, brings the sense of loss to me.
Our broken fates no hope attends. But if on earth we meet no
more,
Await me on that fairy shore behind whose clouds the moon
ascends!
A moulded form whose smooth excess sweet fragrance clung
around.
A dream of rapture magical that made the pulses bound.
Her equal in the court of Han as yet had never been.
What new attire for Yang Kuei-fei to shroud her in the ground?"[1]

Upon reading these verses, the emperor was so overcome that he made the powerful eunuch Kao Li-shih go down on his knees and pull off the poet's boots.[2]

His Majesty ordered the best wine to be served in honour of the occasion and every one emptied cup after cup to add merriment to the festive gathering. The

---

1. Translation by W. J. B. Fletcher.
2. It chanced that upon one occasion a messenger from the Korean emperor arrived at Chang-an with a document written in Korean. There was apparently no one in the capital who could understand the message, and the emperor was much vexed. The President of the Hanlin Academy, Ho Chih-chang (賀知章), as the leading scholar at court, therefore felt upset. On seeing this, Li Po, who was staying with the minister, consoled him by saying that he could translate the document. On receiving this intelligence the emperor ordered the head eunuch Kao Li-shih to invite Li Po to the palace. It was not until after repeated journeys, however, that the poet finally consented to undertake the task and he did this so well that the emperor rewarded him with a high honour. Not long afterwards, when Li Po came into power, he confided to His Majesty the reason for his strange action, for both the eunuch and Yang Kuo-chung were jealous of, and unkind towards him, and even passed such remarks as follows, "Li Po's literary talent is so poor, that he is not worthy of holding my ink-slab" and "He is not worthy enough to pull off my boot." Hence the emperor's curious action.

more Li Po drank, the better he wrote. The emperor himself blew the flute and Kuei-fei accompanied him on the guitar. After midnight Li Po thanked His Majesty and the favourite and retired to his modest quarters at the Hanlin Academy.

On another occasion, the emperor, who was enjoying himself with Kuei-fei in the palace grounds, invited Li Po to commemorate the scene in poetry. After some delay, the poet arrived, supported between two eunuchs. "May it please Your Majesty," he said indistinctly, "I have been dining with the prince and he has made me drunk, but I will do my best." Thereupon two ladies-in-waiting of the court held up in front of him a pink silk screen, and in a very short time he had composed no less than ten eight-line stanzas, from which the following verses, describing the life and extraordinary beauty of the reigning favourite, are quoted:

"Oh, the joy of youth spent in a gold-fretted hall,
In the crepe-flower Pavilion, the fairest of all,
My tresses for head-dress with gay garlands girt
Carnations arranged o'er my jacket and skirt!
Then to wander away in the soft-scented air,
And return by the side of His Majesty's chair —
But the dance and the song will be o'er by and by,
And we shall dislimn like the rack in the sky."[1]

His wild Bohemian life, together with his gay and dissolute career at court, formed a most effec-

---

1. Translation by Herbert A. Giles.

tive setting for the splendid flow of verses which he never ceased to pour forth. His greatest pleasures lay in drinking wine and writing poetry. His fame spread wider then ever, after he entered the palace. The strength of his poetry, as well as his readiness to participate in scenes of revelry and dissipation provided for the amusement of the ever-giddy Kuei-fei, gained for him the emperor's unbounded admiration and good will. His Majesty showered favour after favour upon him, and wished to confer upon him an important post at court, but he politely declined. The envious eunuch Kao Li-shih constantly spoke of him in a disrespectful manner to Kuei-fei. The mean fellow was forever creating trouble and making the poet's prolonged stay in the palace very unpleasant. Li Po was too wise to report the conduct of the powerful attendant to the emperor, as investigation might provoke greater envy. He therefore decided to go home. The emperor sent for him one day and asked him: "Must you really leave me? As you have rendered valuable services to the throne, I cannot let you go home empty-handed." After further entreaties, the emperor sorrowfully gave his consent for Li Po to retire. The mighty ruler presented him with an imperial edict by which the distinguished poet might obtain wine free of charge wherever he travelled. He took full advantage of this extraordinary imperial graciousness, and life was thereafter unending wine and song, until his final retirement into the mountains of his own province.

THE SISTERS' IMITATION
OF KUEI-FEI

IT was customary in China for all the scholars of a certain grade to come to the capital for their examinations, following which different degrees were conferred upon the successful candidates. There were two exceptionally bright young men who had just received their degrees. The first, named Ch'in Kuo-chen (秦國楨), who obtained the highest degree of Chuang Yüan, was exceptionally handsome. One spring afternoon, when nature was at her best, he went round the city to admire the many attractive spots where trees were abundant. The next day he rode on horseback and peeped into a big private garden covered with all kinds of rare trees and flowers. Ch'in Kuo-chen hesitated awhile in rapt admiration of the scene. He then strayed further into the garden, but unfortunately, owing to the tortuous paths, was not able to find his way out. There were many beautiful bridges, artificial hillocks and small pavilions. He imagined that this property must belong to a member of the royal family, otherwise, who could have afforded such luxuries? Having no special permission to enter, he was afraid that he might be taken for a trespasser. While he was pondering what to do, a small maidservant approached him, pulled his coat and invited him to come in for a cup of tea. Ch'in Kuo-chen was alarmed and said, "Please tell me the name of your master." Before he could get a reply there came a dozen fashionably dressed maidens, but the one who walked in the centre was the most attractive of all. At the sight of these ladies, Ch'in Kuo-chen was at a loss for words. He struggled hard to run away, but the young enchantress would not let him go, and insisted upon knowing his personal name. The young graduate pondered for a moment and then gave a false one. Their conversation thus casually begun became more and more animated until it grew dark. The hostess then said, "Is it not strange that last night I dreamt of a handsome hero calling upon me and here I am facing my prince!"

The one thus flattered blushed and could find no words to relieve him from his embarrassment, The maids, realizing this, immediately brought wine and food and every one soon became hilarious. The artful hostess waited until he was completely intoxicated and then made love to him. The night was thus passed amid strange surroundings. Alas for the young man! He forgot his reputation and position and allowed the beauty of a woman to obliterate other thoughts from his mind. Thus, he spent many days in perfect bliss, quite oblivious of everything else. The world of mortals being what it is, and its complexions so far determined by the play of human passion, even the greatest hero or a Son of Heaven feels absolutely helpless before a seductive and beautiful woman.

Meanwhile, the emperor summoned Ch'in Kuo-chen as senior optimus to appear for audience. A search was instituted far and wide for him, but without success. One day, while the entranced scholar and his secret charmer were drinking wine, the latter spoke to him about the mysterious disappearance of a young graduate — Ch'in Kuo-chen by name — and how anxious the emperor was to grant him an interview. Upon hearing this, young Kuo-chen was alarmed. He threw himself at the feet of his hostess and implored her to forgive him for having deceived her, for he himself was the man in question. Unconsciously, her tears fell and she said, "Fate has brought us together, but we must soon part." Ch'in Kuo-chen replied: "Such love as ours will enable us to meet again some day. Pray give me your name so that I may always cherish your fond memory."

"As my lord is away," resumed the fair one, "I cannot tell you his name just now. If you do not forget

my love, there is always a way to bring us together."
She then handed him a small water colour painting of
herself and said: "When you meet His Majesty show
him this picture and tell him that on your way you met a
fairy who entertained you with banquets every evening,
and that she was the cause of your delay in coming. If
you convey these words to His Majesty, he will surely
pardon you." In this mood Ch'in Kuo-chen parted from
his lover amid tears and fond embraces.

At the audience with his sovereign the young lover
repeated exactly the words the lady had told him. He
then took out the portrait from his sleeve and nervously
showed it. The emperor instantly recognized it as that
of Kuei-fei's youngest sister, and, laughing heartily,
said: "This girl reminds me of Kuei-fei's three sisters.
They are equally beautiful and independent girls, but
the youngest one is the most charming and frivolous of
all. She often lures young and handsome men, and
conceals them in her residence to enjoy happiness with
her. These sisters visit the court every day. They love
adventure."

The emperor supplied each of Kuei-fei's sisters
with a thousand taels of silver as their monthly allow-
ance. He pampered to all their whims and built attractive mansions inside the imperial city for them. Their
palatial establishments were replete with every comfort
and luxury. The youngest one was the emperor's
favourite sister-in-law. She was an exceedingly sen-

suous young widow, and may be likened to a modern vampire. She needed no make-up for her complexion, though she might now and then lightly touch her eyebrows with a little carbon black. Her skin had a natural rosy hue. Daily she rode on her pony round the imperial courtyard unchaperoned! This was a privilege to which only the emperor was entitled. She dared break the convention, because she relied on Kuei-fei's influence. Hundreds of spectators paid more attention to her frivolous exploits than to any pomp at court.

One day, when the apple and plum trees were in full bloom and the garden looked like a paradise, Kuei-fei and her sisters planned a stroll in the garden. The emperor made a sign with his eyes to the youngest sister-in-law, who thereupon excused herself by saying to Kuei-fei, "You go ahead, I shall join you as soon as I have changed into neater costume." But she purposely stayed behind, so that the emperor was able to enjoy the liberty of making love to her alone. When Kuei-fei heard about this incident she was enraged at the temerity of her sister and her sovereign lord. She wept freely, kept herself aloof, and would not talk for several days. Such notorious scandals as the above characterized the later court life during the reign of the Ming Huang. Jealous by nature, Kuei-fei was not a woman to tolerate lightly a rebuff where her individual happiness was concerned. She did not try to conceal her displeasure. Her feelings towards her royal lover became strained, and he paid dearly for the tears she shed. It took her many months to forget it. Her slightest whim was law in the palace thereafter. To atone for his frivolities, the foolish sovereign ordered more banquets accompanied by further revelries.

THE SUMMER RESORT

HE white parrot, named Snowdress Maiden (雪衣女) *(hsüeh i nü)*, presented by An Lu-shan to the emperor, who passed it on to Kuei-fei, soon became a great favourite in the palace. Kuei-fei was exceedingly fond of it, and the bird could be seen constantly by her side. Being unchained, it flew about freely in the spacious grounds. It learnt all sorts of words and phrases, and appeared almost human in its ability to say the right thing at the right time.

After a few years the parrot sickened and died. This event marked a sorrowful chapter in Kuei-fei's life, for she was extremely attached to it. She ordered a special chased silver casket for its body, and buried it in a prominent corner of the palace garden. She even chanted Buddhist songs for the peace of her dead companion. The emperor himself was much touched by this attachment, and liberated fifty parrots in the palace as a sign of imperial good will.

This incident occurred about the time of An Lu-shan's departure for his distant post, and the yearning for her secret lover, coupled with the loss of her parrot was responsible for her somewhat morose temperament during later years. It also accounted for the emperor's decision to remove to the new Hua-ch'ing Palace (華清宮), where the shameful revelries and orgies to be described later on took place. At any rate, her attachment to the parrot revealed a more human and sympathetic side of Kuei-fei's character.

After the incident cited in the last chapter, the emperor was constantly thinking of new ways of pleasing his indispensable favourite, and had therefore scant leisure for attending to the affairs of state. He reasoned that if he should stay in the palace, he would have to get up at day-break and hold audience every morning. If he should neglect his duty, the officials would complain. The best way, therefore, to avoid all responsibilities was to leave the court for a while, and devote more time to private enjoyment. The emperor, therefore, accompanied by Kuei-fei and hundreds of court ladies, maidservants and eunuchs, left for Hua-ch'ing Palace, a famous summer resort some leagues away. In this delightful retreat, a running stream bridged with elaborately modelled arches, wound its way through a landscape of miniature hills, topped by high pagodas. In the near vicinity, under the deep shade cast by clusters of trees, were placed chairs and seats of carved marble, offering a cool retreat from which to enjoy the beauties of the flower garden. Lotus flowers covered the lake, and the lovely zigzag paths afforded continuous pleasure to poet, artist and lover. There were sixteen bathing ponds provided for the court ladies. The most attractive was an imperial pool where the emperor and Kuei-fei enjoyed their daily bath. It was constructed of white marble surrounded by ornamental stone-carved birds. The finer parts were mounted with precious stones and rubies. The fountain was noted for its perennial warmth even in the springtime. On moonlight nights, the emperor and Kuei-fei would go and bathe together.

In a famous poem, this holiday of the two imperial lovers is thus described:

" 'Twas in the chilly springtime,
    They bathed in Hua-ch'ing Lake;
  And in the tepid waters
    The crusted winter slake.

"When thence attendants bore her,
    So flawless and so fair;
  Then strong beat in her prince's breast
    Desire and tender care."

The emperor would give his companion her bath and gently rub her delicate skin. During these days of content, they would put on simple clothes and undertake boating excursions upon the lake. His Majesty endeavoured to please Kuei-fei with humorous bantering and much flattery. The musicians and dancing girls followed them whenever necessary. Thus they turned day into night, and night into day.

At last autumn approached. The ministers sent numerous petitions begging the emperor to return without delay to the capital and attend to urgent state affairs. Nevertheless, the enraptured sovereign lingered on. The happy hours and days sped on in one continuous whirl of excitement and merriment.

Chapter Sixteen

A MIDNIGHT VOW

N the seventh day of the seventh moon, when everything was quiet and the attendants at Hua-ch'ing Palace had all retired, the emperor and Kuei-fei went strolling unaccompanied in the garden and entered the Hall of Immortality (長生殿). The crescent-shaped moon was unusually bright, and they sat up until two o'clock in the morning, watching the clear sky and searching for the Milky Way, commonly believed to be most visible on that particular evening. The emperor whispered into his beloved's ear: "People say that to-night the shepherd boy meets his fairy wife. Their happiness must be boundless."[1]

---

1. This refers to the old Chinese legend and play entitled "Tien Ho P'ei" (天河配), In that legend the romantic story is related of the shepherd boy who meets his fairy wife once a year on the seventh day of the seventh month.

Kuei-fei replied, with an affected sigh: "Heavenly happiness is everlasting, but happiness on earth is never permanent, for no matter how contented we may be now, we can never tell when one may be separated from the other." At these words, the emperor was greatly moved. He drew Kuei-fei closer, embraced her most tenderly, and pointing to the bright stars above solemnly pledged: "My dearest one, we have loved each other for nearly twenty years. Has the world ever seen such an attachment as ours? I swear that we will ever fly like the one-winged birds, or grow united like the tree with branches which twine together. Heaven and earth may pass away, but our love shall last forever." Kuei-fei was immensely pleased. She thanked the emperor and also pointing to the star-lit sky to be their witness, uttered the same vow.

In the ninth moon of that year, the orange trees were full of fruit, an event rather unusual and too early for the season. The emperor expressed much delight and regarded this incident as a happy omen of the future. He plucked one orange, gave half to Kuei-fei to eat and exclaimed, "Is it not strange that these trees seem to understand the sacred vow we made at the Hall of Immortality?" To commemorate this occasion, he ordered the whole palace to be lighted up with red lanterns, the radiant hue and soft glow from which helped to transform the entire atmosphere into a veritable dream city.

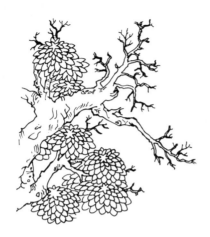

Chapter Seventeen

FINAL GAIETIES IN
THE PALACE

OON after their return from Hua-ch'ing Palace, the imperial residence was completely re-decorated. Hundreds of beautiful embroidered garments were made for Kuei-fei by the court ladies. Presents of every description from the imperial clans, as well as from distant and near officials, poured into the court to celebrate her birthday. Sumptuous theatricals and feastings were held in her honour for several days, the best musicians in the capital were engaged, and promotions were conferred upon many dignitaries. Kuei-fei requested the musicians to play a song entitled "The Rainbow Skirt and Feather Jacket," which she had composed herself. She often put on rainbow-coloured garments and danced with the light-ness and grace of a fairy during the banquets. In the eyes of the princes, princesses and other courtiers her many accomplishments were unrivalled. The court had never seen Kuei-fei dance more charmingly. Her speciality on this occasion was the mounting of a round table on which she skilfully performed a classic turn comparable to the Bacchanalian dance of ancient Europe. Her wonderful skill and art so fascinated the emperor, that he classed her among the immortal fairies. In his absorbed and besotted mind, no being, human or spiritual, could approach his heart's love in such grace and perfection. So devoted was His Majesty that he ever wished her to appear alongside of him in the imperial chariot. Sometimes she would ride on horseback, with the chief eunuch and maids escorting her, and the emperor riding by her side. Hundreds of court ladies waited eagerly to pay their daily homage to the august sovereign and his favourite. His Majesty enjoyed himself in the society of these ladies, drinking with them, listening to their music, or strolling with them through the beautiful gardens. He was in favour of continuing the daily feastings and theatricals at all costs. Kuei-fei and her three sisters were thus led into paths of unheard-of extravagances and sensual dissipation. They were daily wafted to ecstasy and transported with joy over the winecups of the banquet-hall. Alas, the whole country was burning, but the sovereign not only fiddled, but danced to his own obscene music! While province after province passed through fire and sword to uphold the sway of the falling ruler, he was still thoughtlessly busying himself with new amusements for his countless maidens, or joining his evil genius, the notorious Yang Kuo-chung, in unspeakable orgies and debauchery. The pleasure-loving sovereign remained in blissful ignorance of his country's impending disaster, dwelling contentedly in a court riddled with corruption and fast living.

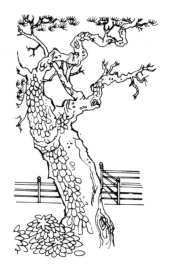

THE EMPEROR IN
A CRITICAL SITUATION

AN LU-SHAN, aiming at the overthrow of the throne that he might possess Kuei-fei to himself, has been secretly scheming against the emperor. Through the influence of Kuei-fei and the unworthy Prime Minister Li Lin-fu (李林甫), he held the military governorship of three frontier cities for a long time. Gradually he replaced all the Chinese officials under him with savage Tartars.

Consequently in A.D. 754 China failed in an attempt to reduce the Tartar state of Nan-chao (南詔). This so weakened the military strength of the empire that An Lu-shan at once seized the opportunity to enter into a conspiracy with the wild hordes, leading ultimately to a wide-spread rebellion.

When news reached the court of An Lu-shan's

suspected treachery, the emperor summoned his ministers and informed them that, in view of the serious condition of the state, he would himself become generalissimo and lead the forces, as of old, against the rebel forces.

As soon as Yang Kuo-chung heard this, he hastened to consult his cousin Kuei-fei, as their careers and even lives would be jeopardized, should His Majesty discover the rotten and corrupt condition of the army.

Kuei-fei pondered long over the matter, and finally said she had a plan ready to save the situation.

Towards evening, when the emperor adjourned to his favourite's apartments, he found her hair dishevelled, her head ornaments scattered about, her mouth filled with yellow earth, and her eyes wet with tears. On His Majesty's asking for the cause, Kuei-fei replied: "I have just learnt that my august lord is leaving the capital to take the field himself. How can I help being miserable and anxious, knowing well the dangers ahead of thee? These rumours of An Lu-shan's treachery are all idle, spread by mischief-makers to mislead Thy Majesty and lure thee away. In all the six palaces, I am the Son of Heaven's most-favoured one. For years I have been thy loving and devoted slave. I cannot bear to leave thy side for even a day. Being a mere woman I regret that I cannot follow my lord to share glory in thy victory. I would therefore rather break my head against the ground to show my love and gratitude to my sovereign master.''

On hearing this appeal the emperor's heart melted. He raised Kuei-fei from the ground, petted her and said: "For over forty years I have governed this land, and have gone through bitter experiences. Now I am sick of power and glory, and wish nothing better than to retire and pass the throne to my heir apparent. Thou and I will retire to another palace and enjoy the rest of our lives together. Will that suit thee better, my dearest?"

At this unexpected reply to her crafty appeal, Kuei-fei became frightened, as she did not wish to lose her present power (for the emperor's retirement would certainly bring this about). She replied: "Last autumn, Thy Majesty had already considered abdication, but could not then bear to expose the prince to danger. There is now more reason than ever not to expose him. Thy Majesty has reigned twoscore years and has had rare success and experience. In these critical times, thou surely canst not wish to leave the state in danger, but wilt wait until the present troubles are over."

The emperor slowly considered the matter and said: "Thou art right, my love. I will not leave thee or my capital." He then appointed some of his ablest generals to undertake the task of subjugating the rebels, and ordered the maids to fetch Kuei-fei's best clothing, and robe her. Feasting and music then fol-

71

lowed far into the night. By thus giving into his favourite on a question of the supremest importance, the emperor hastened the day of his downfall.

The disturbances throughout the land continued, and the rebel forces gradually approached the capital. After Liao-yang (略陽), the eastern metropolis, had been invaded and taken by storm, An Lu-shan usurped the title of emperor and proclaimed his newly conquered territory the state of Yen (燕). The next fortress, against which he directed his forces, was T'ung-kuan (潼關). The capital Chang-an was defended by Ko Shuhan (哥舒翰), a distinguished general, whose plan was to avoid an encounter with the enemy until Kuo Tzu-yi (郭子儀) and Li Kuang-pi (李光弼), governors of Suofang (朔方) and Ho-pei (河北) respectively, had had time to march against P'ing-lu (平盧), the stronghold of the rebel forces. In spite of these precautions, General Ko eventually fell into the hands of the victorious rebels. After T'ung-kuan fell, there was nothing to prevent the invaders from marching directly upon the capital city.

By this time, the violent measures of An Lu-shan had roused a storm of indignation everywhere. Numerous messages reached the capital warning the emperor of An Lu-shan's duplicity. The hitherto careless monarch was at last undeceived, and turned his attention to the necessitous condition of his subjects. He proposed to issue orders preventing further bloodshed. He said to Kuei-fei: "An Lu-shan is indeed a treacherous and ungrateful fellow. You and I have treated him too well. His uncontrollable greed and love of power have wrecked my nation." Kuei-fei bent her head low and said nothing.

The situation changed from bad to worse, hour by hour, with such rapidity, that the city was soon in a stormy tumult. At the height of the crisis, the emperor, realizing that the enemy forces were nearing the capital, became immensely worried. Kuei-fei and her kinsmen approached him in tears and begged him to save the situation. So great was the alarm of the monarch that he finally decided to evacuate the palace. Accompanied by the prince, Kuei-fei, her sisters, Yang Kuo-chung, the eunuch Kao Li-shih and a dozen personal attendants, the emperor set out at day-break. Before quitting the last gate, the emperor suddenly remembered Mei-fei and wanted to bring her along too, but Kuei-fei protested stubbornly, saying, "If Your Majesty saves her, I will stay behind and let the enemy kill me". The emperor was thus prevented from performing a last kindly act to his early love.

Chapter Nineteen

THE TRAGIC END

IT was the summer of the year A.D. 756. The air was unusually dry and sultry. Before the break of dawn, the noise of the frightened masses could be heard in the distance, some in faint, prolonged cries, others in sharp, shrieking notes. The dew was still heavy on the ground, the dragon robe was soaked, the whole nation's fate rested upon the shoulders of the Son of Heaven. The bodies of the dead littered the roadside and floated on ponds. Men, women, and helpless children huddled together in the streets. Thousands of innocent people, old and young alike, had been slain. On arrival at Ma-wei (馬嵬), the soldiers forming the emperor's escort mutinied, and killed Yang Kuo-chung, the unpopular courtier. On hearing this, the distressed monarch approached the front gate and en-

74

treated his soldiers to obey orders and protect his sacred person. The mutineers, however, refused to advance against the enemy and presented a counter-demand, namely, the life of Kuei-fei. "We are not afraid to die," they clamoured, "but we must first kill the hated woman, for she is entirely responsible for this calamity to our nation."

When he heard these words, the emperor was terrified. His face turned pale and he said in a tremulous voice, "But Kuei-fei only lived in the Forbidden City and never meddled with state affairs." The general-in-charge and the head eunuch then prostrated themselves in front of him and in tears cried: "Your Majesty, this is true, but the situation is helpless. Unless the life of your beloved consort is sacrificed, even the safety of your precious person may not be guaranteed." The sovereign, realizing now that no power on earth could save Kuei-fei, experienced the most agonizing grief. He lingered for a long while, uncertain what steps to take, for he had not the heart to enter the inner court. Seeing his indecision, the chief eunuch again fell upon his knees and beseeched the distracted monarch not to hesitate further. Roused as if from a trance, Ming Huang at last dragged his tired limbs into the inner chamber and for a moment disappeared from the view of the soldiers. Then, leading the trembling Kuei-fei out by the hand, he exclaimed passionately: "My dearest, I cannot believe that the hour has come when I must perforce leave you for ever and suffer you to perish in this wise. Oh, why has Heaven deserted us so cruelly?"

With dishevelled hair and torn and soiled garments, Kuei-fei knelt down and wept. "Your humble wife has indeed sinned," she said. "To suffer death is no regret. I beseech Your Majesty to take care of yourself. But first allow me to pray to my god Buddha before meeting the fate in store for me." To this the emperor replied, "Oh, I beseech Heaven that my dearly beloved be re-incarnated on the lotus throne."

He then commanded Kao Li-shih to minister carefully to her needs until the end. Next, he covered his face with the wide sleeves of his yellow imperial robe, and as he turned back experienced the utmost despair, feeling as if the whole world had deserted him.

Kuei-fei herself entertained a sense of being cruelly wronged. She was thirsting for some deeper draught of life than had yet befallen her lot. By the tragic irony of fate, she was obliged to face premature death instead. Aloud she cried in lamentation:

"The flowers are withered, the rain is falling,
The bright moon is hidden behind the clouds;
For we who are one in soul are to be separated;
I recall with agonizing memory our vows at the Hall of Immortality.
The bird has lost one of its wings,
Alone in the grave I must lie,
My soul is in agony, my spirit sore wounded,

Is there no merciful compassion for me?
Ask thyself, my Lord?
At eighteen I entered the palace,
And for twenty years I rejoiced in thy favours,
But today I am sent to death alone:
My tears are blinding my eyes,
What desolation, what distress, that my body
Should thus hang from the tree alone!"

She then rolled in agony on the ground. The whole world was forsaking her. The war drums were sounding louder and louder as if the earth was trembling.

Her eyes streaming with tears, Kuei-fei slowly but steadily ascended the steps leading to the shrine of Buddha, and prostrated herself before the beneficent god. In the spacious compound stood an old pear tree with overhanging branches. A finely carved round stool of brown oak was already there. Kao Li-shih, the faithful eunuch, knelt down before Kuei-fei and handed her a long silken cord for her to commit the final act. Without undue delay, for the shouts of the surrounding soldiers were becoming more and more threatening, she stepped upon the stool, passed the cord over a strong branch of the pear tree, slipped it round her neck and thus hanged herself. In a few minutes life was extinct, and the notorious Kuei-fei — most famous of Chinese historical women, unchallenged consort of a weak though kind-hearted monarch for two whole decades, and the virtual ruler of ancient China for nearly a quarter of a century — was no more.

As soon as the soldiers perceived that Kuei-fei was dead, they knelt down and acclaimed, "Long live the spirit of Her Highness!" The desolate emperor, outwardly defiant, though inwardly grief-stricken, poured out passionate words to his attendant Kao Li-shih: "Oh, bring back the soul of my beloved Kuei-fei to me! I have nothing to live for now, but to dream of her day and night and to pray that I may soon join her in the other world."

The soldiers returned to their allegiance and escorted their broken-hearted sovereign to the palace. Soon afterwards he abdicated in favour of his son, who was proclaimed emperor with the title of Su-tsung (肅 宗) in Ling-wu (靈 武, now Ling-chow 靈州, Kansu). This brought to a close the forty-five years of Ming Huang's reign which commenced in A.D. 712 when the emperor was at the youthful age of twenty-seven.

CHAPTER
TWENTY

THE SPIRIT OF KUEI-FEI
RETURNS

TWO long weary years passed. After repeated invitations from his son, who had taken his place as emperor, the aged Ming Huang, now past his seventy-first birthday, decided to visit the scene of his former triumphs. As he traversed the green verdure and imposing valleys of Szechwan province on his way to the capital, he heaved frequent sighs and longed for the return of the old days when his heart's joy was constantly at his side. When the once familiar hills of Ma-wei came into view, a pang of remorse and longing smote his heart. For a moment he half expected to see again the lovely form of Kuei-fei whom these scenes recalled, but, instead, his mind pictured with bitter remembrance that tragic scene of final separation. He now turned eastward towards the imperial city where his former ministers were waiting for him. Both parties understood their innermost sorrows, and their robes were wet with tears. There stood the same T'ai Yeh (lotus lake) with the beautiful garden adjoining, and the same imposing trees lining the walls. Everything in the garden appeared the same as of yore. At that moment Ming Huang recalled the lotus-like face of his beloved and her graceful eyebrows, curved like the willows when bent by a passing wind. The sight of these palace scenes reminded him of the happy past, and tears flowed down in abundant streams from his eyes.

Autumn had now set in. The *wutung* leaves had turned brown and fallen upon the unswept yard of the west palace. The hair of the "pear orchard" musicians had turned grey, while the eunuchs and maids appeared to have pined away. The ex-emperor trimmed his lamp night after night, meanwhile dreaming of his dead consort. He could almost hear the unceasing sound of the watch-drums, but never once did her spirit come to soothe him in his misery.

One day, so the story goes, a wandering Taoist priest, from Lin-ch'ung district in Szechwan, arrived at Chang-an city as an honored guest of the Hung-tu governor. He possessed the rare magic power of calling departed spirits back. Ming Huang commanded this man to appear before him, and poured out to him all his sorrows and longings, from beginning to end. When the emperor had finished, the priest said he was confident he could reincarnate the spirit of Kuei-fei for

Ming Huang, but only on condition that he should fast for seven whole days and not cry or lament when they were face to face. To this the sad monarch eagerly agreed. Then, like lightning, the soul of the priest flitted away to the nether regions in order to seek the spirit of Kuei-fei. After many fruitless searches from the highest heaven to the lowest earth, he heard of an Isle of the Blest, away in mid-ocean, lying as if unsupported in the open azure space. There, within high glinting towers and gaily decorated buildings, dwelt in peace numberless immortals, fair and beautiful. The loveliest among these was called T'ai-chen, whom he took to be the spirit of Kuei-fei.

The Taoist priest then hied thither and alighted. He knocked at a door on the western side of the golden palace and informed the attendant that Han Huang (i.e., Ming Huang) was longing to see T'ai-chen on earth. On hearing the glad tidings, T'ai-chen awoke from her dream, pushed her pillows aside, and raised the curtains. Quickly she clad herself and went into the hall. Her hair was somewhat disarranged, but kept in position with a glowing garland of pearls. Her flowing garments were blown about by the wind and assumed the multi-coloured appearance of the rainbow. She looked refreshed and fair after her sleep. Her face seemed wistful and sad, and tears obscured her eyes. She thanked the messenger for the emperor's love and care, and exclaimed: "Does His Majesty know what I have gone through since we parted in the mortal world? When I turn my gaze upon this earth inhabited by man, I can only see dear Chang-an city covered with mist and wreaths. Our old love at Chao-yang court has been cruelly severed, but as the sun and moon shine everlastingly over the fairy palace, so surely our affection shall ever remain eternally. To show you that I am really his old love, see me break in twain this clasp and this bracelet, which His Majesty presented me years ago. Take back to him half of each and urge him to be firm at heart, so that we may meet again in immortal Heaven. When returning them to him, remind my lord of the vow made by him and me on the seventh day of the seventh moon at the Hall of Immortality, in which we consecrated our supreme love and gave our oath to live and to die together. Heaven is vast, the earth is old, time will pass away, but this great wrong shall last for ever and ever."

With this thrilling message, the priest returned to the grief-stricken sovereign. The latter could scarcely believe the news until shown the clasp and bracelet, and finally was reminded of his midnight tryst on the seventh day of the seventh moon, which nobody but he and Kuei-fei were supposed to have known.

Then he begged to be allowed to see the spirit of Kuei-fei, and willingly carried out the necessary fast. At last the meeting took place, the aged lover watching from afar the incomparable and unforgettable face of his queen in ethereal form — motionless and speechless, but undoubtedly the image of his departed love.

Try as he would, he could not restrain from utter-
ing a moan or his tears from flowing down, and lo, in a
moment, the apparition had gone, and he woke up to
find himself again in his lonely surroundings.

FINIS

APPENDIX
THE EVERLASTING WRONG[1]

Poem by Po Chu-i (A.D. 772–846), translated by H. H. Giles

Ennui. — His Imperial Majesty, a slave to beauty,
        longed for a "Subverter of Empires";[2]
    For years he had sought in vain
        to secure such a treasure for his palace. . . .

Beauty. — From the Yang family came a maiden,
        just grown up to womanhood,
    Reared in the inner apartments,
        altogether unknown to fame.
    But nature had amply endowed her
        with a beauty hard to conceal,
    And one day she was summoned
        to a place at the monarch's side.
    Her sparkling eye and merry laughter
        fascinated every beholder,
    And among the powder and paint of the harem
        her loveliness reigned supreme.
    In the chills of spring, by imperial mandate,
        she bathed in the Hua-ch'ing Pool,
    Laving her body in the glassy wavelets
        of the fountain perennially warm.
    Then, when she came forth, helped by attendants,
        her delicate and graceful movements
    Finally gained for her gracious favour,
        captivating His Majesty's heart.

---

1. "Chinese Literature," W. Heinemann, London, 1901.
2. Referring to a famous beauty of the Han dynasty, one glance from whom would overthrow a city, two glances an empire.

Revelry. — Hair like a cloud, face like a flower,
      head-dress which quivered as she walked,
Amid the delights of the Hibiscus Pavilion
      she passed the soft spring nights,
Spring nights, too short alas! for them,
      albeit prolonged till dawn, —
From this time forth no more audiences
      in the hours of early morn.
Revels and feasts in quick succession,
      ever without a break,
She chosen always for the spring excursion,
      chosen for the nightly carouse.
Three thousand peerless beauties adorned
      the apartments of the monarch's harem,
Yet always His Majesty reserved
      his attentions for her alone.
Passing her life in a "golden house,"[1]
      with fair girls to wait on her,
She was daily wafted to ecstasy
      on the wine fumes of the banquet-hall.
Her sisters and her brothers, one and all,
      were raised to the rank of nobles.
Alas! for the ill-omened glories
For thus it came about that fathers and mothers
      through the length and breadth of the empire
Rejoiced no longer over the birth of sons,
      but over the birth of daughters.
In the gorgeous palace
      piercing the grey clouds above,

---

1. Referring to A-chiao, one of the consorts of an emperor of the Han dynasty. "Ah," said the latter when a boy, "if I could only get A-chiao, I would have a golden house to keep her in."

Divine music, borne on the breeze,
    is spread around on all sides;
Of song and the dance
    to the guitar and flute,
All through the live long day,
    His Majesty never tires.
But suddenly comes the roll
    of the fishskin war-drums,
Breaking rudely upon the air
    of the "Rainbow Skirt and Feather Jacket."

Flight. — Clouds of dust envelope
    the lofty gates of the capital.
A thousand warchariots and ten thousand horses
    move towards the south-west.
Feathers and jewels among the throng,
    onwards and then a halt.
A hundred li beyond the western gate,
    leaving behind them the city walls,
The soldiers refuse to advance;
    nothing remains to be done
Until she of the moth-eyebrows
    perishes in sight of all.
On the ground lie gold ornaments
    with no one to pick them up,
Kingfisher wings, golden birds,
    and hairpins of costly jade.
The monarch covers his face,
    powerless to save;
And as he turns to look back,
    tears and blood flow mingled together.

Exile. — Across vast stretches of yellow sand
    with whistling winds,

Across cloud-capped mountain-tops
    they make their way.
Few indeed are the travellers
    who reached the heights of Mount Omi;
The bright gleam of the standards
    glows fainter day by day.
Dark the Ssŭch'uan waters,
    dark the Ssŭch'uan hills;
Daily and nightly His Majesty
    is consumed by bitter grief.
Travelling along, the very brightness
    of the moon saddens his heart,
And the sound of a bell through the evening rain
    severs his viscera in twain.

Return. — Time passes, days go by, and once again
    he is there at the well-known spot,
And there he lingers on, unable
    to tear himself wholly away.
But from the clods of earth
    at the foot of Ma-wei hill,
No sign of her lovely face appears,
    only the place of death.
The eyes of sovereign and minister meet,
    and robes are wet with tears,
Eastward they depart and hurry on
    to the capital at full speed.

Home. — There is the pool and there are the flowers,
    as of old.
There is the hibiscus of the pavilion,
    there are the willows of the palace.
In the hibiscus he sees her face,
    in the willow he sees her eyebrows;

How in the presence of these
    should tears not flow, —
In spring amid the flowers
    of the peach and plum,
In autumn rains when the leaves
    of the *wu-t'ung* fall?
To the south of the western palace
    are many trees,
And when their leaves cover the steps,
    no one now sweeps them away.
The hair of the Pear-Garden musicians,
    is white as though with age;
The guardians of the Pepper Chamber[1]
    seem to him no longer young.
Where fireflies flit through the hall,
    he sits in silent grief;
Alone, the lamp-wick burnt out,
    he is still unable to sleep.
Slowly pass the watches,
    for the nights are now too long,
And brightly shine the constellations,
    as though dawn would never come.
Cold settles upon the duck-and-drake tiles,[2]
    and thick hoar-frost,
The kingfisher coverlet is chill,
    with none to share its warmth.
Parted by life and death,
    time still goes on,
But never once does her spirit come back
    to visit him in dreams.

---

1. A fancy name for the women's apartments in the palace.
2. The mandarin duck and drake are emblems of conjugal fidelity. The allusion is to ornaments on the roof.

Spirit-land. — A Taoist priest of Lin-ch'ung,
      of the Hung-tu school,
Was able, by his perfect art, to summon
      the spirits of the dead.
Anxious to relieve the fretting mind
      of his sovereign,
This magician receives orders
      to urge a diligent quest.
Borne on the clouds, charioted upon ether,
      he rushes with the speed of lightning
High up to heaven, low down to earth,
      seeking everywhere.
Above, he searches the empyrean;
      below, the Yellow Springs,
But nowhere in these vast areas
      can her place be found.
At length he hears of an Isle of the Blest
      away in mid-ocean,
Lying in realms of vacuity,
      dimly to be descried.
There gaily decorated buildings
      rise up like rainbow clouds,
And there many gentle and beautiful Immortals
      pass their days in peace.
Among them is one whose name
      sounds upon lips as Eternal,
And by her snow-white skin and flower-like
      face he knows that this is she.
Knocking at the jade door
      at the western gate of the golden palace,
He bids a fair waiting-maid announce him
      to her mistress, fairer still.
She, hearing of this embassy

sent by the Son of Heaven,
Starts up from her dreams
    among the tapestry curtains.
Grasping her clothes and pushing away the
    pillow, she arises in haste,
And begins to adorn herself
    with pearls and jewels.
Her cloud-like coiffure, dishevelled,
    shows that she has just risen from sleep,
And with her flowery head-dress awry,
    she passes into the hall.
The sleeves of her immortal robes
    are filled out by the breeze,
As once more she seems to dance
    to the "Rainbow Skirt and Feather Jacket."
Her features are fixed and calm,
    though myriad tears fall,
Wetting a spray of pear-bloom,
    as it were with the raindrops of spring.
Subduing her emotions, restraining her grief,
    she tenders thanks to His Majesty,
Saying how since they parted
    she has missed his form and voice;
And how, although their love on earth
    has so soon come to an end,
The days and months among the Blest
    are still of long duration.
And now she turns and gazes
    towards the abode of mortals,
But cannot discern the Imperial city
    lost in the dust and haze.
Then she takes out the old keepsakes,
    tokens of undying love,

A gold hairpin, an enamel brooch,
    and bids the magician carry these back.
One half of the hairpin she keeps,
    and one half of the enamel brooch,
Breaking with her hands the yellow gold,
    and dividing the enamel in two.
"Tell him," she said, "to be firm of heart,
    as this gold and enamel,
And then in Heaven or on earth below
    we two may meet once more."
At parting, she confided to the magician
    many earnest messages of love,
Among the rest recalling a pledge
    mutually understood;
How on the seventh day of the seventh moon,
    ·in the Hall of Immortality,
At midnight, when none were near,
    he had whispered in her ear,
"I swear that we will ever fly
    like the one-winged birds,[1]
Or grow united like the tree
    with branches which twine together."[2]
Heaven and earth, long-lasting as they are,
    will some day pass away;
But this great wrong shall stretch out for ever,
    endless, for ever and ay.

---

1. Each bird having only one wing, must always fly with a mate.
2. Such a tree was believed to exist, and has often been figured by the Chinese.